D0430904

Anna Helm Baxter
photography by Victoria Wall Harris

68 RECIPES FOR
SALADS AND DRESSINGS

TEN SPEED PRESS
Berkeley

CONTENTS

INTRODUCTION

In a world where many of us find ourselves eating meals on the go or at our desks, there seem to be two dismal scenarios. A packed salad that ends up soggy, brown, and limp leafed (or worse, spilled all over your bag). Or an overpriced, mediocre purchased salad that leaves you thinking that you could have done it better (and cheaper) yourself.

Enter the humble jar

Who would have thought that storing salads in a jar could make lunch on the go so much fresher, easier, and cheaper? Tossing a jar of salad in your bag will no longer be like playing a game of lunchtime roulette. Jars keep salad ingredients fresher for longer and make salads more portable, more convenient, and leak-proof. And they are built-in portion control.

Far from the prawn cocktail of my youth, these salads range from the slight to the substantial. The big-jar recipes are packed with whole grains, proteins, and hearty vegetables to keep you out of the snack drawer until dinner. The small-jar recipes are full of flavor with a sprinkling of lighter grains—perfect for less-hungry days or as side dishes.

All of the salad recipes are nutritionally sound, incorporating lots of fresh vegetables, heart-healthy fats, and whole grains so that eating salad feels like a meal rather than a starter course.

What are you waiting for? Happy salad jarring!

Equipment

Very little equipment is needed to assemble salad in jars, but here are a few useful items that will speed up your prep time and make your salad-in-jars experience the best it can be.

- *Wide-mouthed jars* These will make assembling and eating much easier.

- *Salad spinner* Use to get salad greens clean and dry.

- *Y peeler* Use for shaving long ribbons of vegetables.

- *Mandoline or handheld slicer* Use for extra-thin slicing or julienning.

- *Long-handled rubber spatula* Use for getting every last drop of dressing.

Prep times

Some of the recipes call for precooked grains; the cooking guide on page 10 will direct you. Leftover cooked grains can be frozen in zip-top bags, making it simple to pull out what you need, when you need it.

DESIGN YOUR OWN SALAD IN A JAR

The correct layering of ingredients is key to salad success. Dressings should always go on the bottom, followed by ingredients that benefit from marinating in the dressing, such as onions and fennel. Unless you plan on eating the salad that day, ingredients that will go soft, such as croutons and nuts, should be separated by a square of parchment paper right at the top, and fresh fruits should be added on the day you plan to eat the salad. In addition, to keep your salads fresh and increase their shelf life, pack the jars tightly and make sure that all your leaves are very dry before adding them to the jar.

1. The first layer
To keep your salad components from wilting and going soggy, dressings should always go at the bottom. For small jars, I recommend 1 to 2 tablespoons of dressing, and for the big jars, 2 to 4 tablespoons. Oils solidify when refrigerated, so bring your salad to room temperature before trying to shake or dumping it out.

2. The second layer
The second layer in the jar should be hard, crunchy veggies that benefit from marinating and softening in the dressing. Think all types of onions, fennel, whole or halved cherry tomatoes, and carrots. Some pulses, such as lentils and chickpeas, work well in the second layer, too, but these should be fully coated in the dressing so that they absorb it evenly.

3. The third layer
Heavier grains, such as rice, barley, or wheat berries, should be added next. This way they won't weigh down the lighter ingredients. If your salad doesn't include grains, add beans, pasta, or extra veggies here.

4. The fourth layer
If you plan to eat the salad within 24 hours, add proteins (such as fish or chicken), hard-boiled eggs, or heavier cheeses (such as feta) on top of the grains. You can also add an additional layer of veggies here.

5. The fifth layer
Softer fruits and veggies go well here. Think roasted sweet potato or squash, avocado, strawberries, mango, or sliced tomatoes (if they weren't already added in the second layer). Because of their high water content and acidity, it's best to add soft fruits the same day you plan to eat the salad.

6. The sixth layer
Lighter grains like quinoa or couscous should go here. Or, if you have already added a heavy grain, this is where to add your lighter greens.

7. The seventh layer
Lighter greens, such as lettuce, arugula, and baby spinach, should be added here. Or try something new—beet greens, collards, kale, Swiss chard, microgreens, and sprouts all pack much more nutritional punch than your everyday lettuce.

8. The eighth layer
Lighter cheeses, such as Parmesan shavings, should be added here, as well as nuts, croutons, or seeds, separated by a square of parchment.

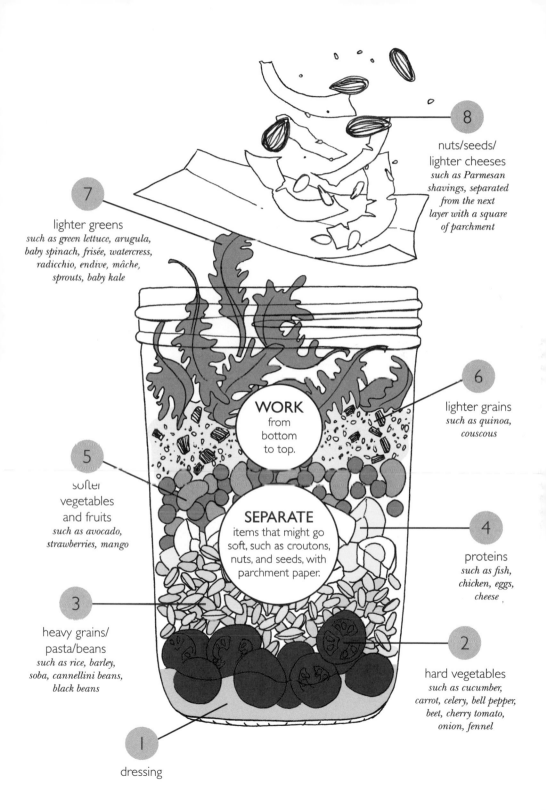

8

nuts/seeds/
lighter cheeses
*such as Parmesan
shavings, separated
from the next
layer with a square
of parchment*

7

lighter greens
*such as green lettuce, arugula,
baby spinach, frisée, watercress,
radicchio, endive, mâche,
sprouts, baby kale*

WORK
from
bottom
to top.

6

lighter grains
*such as quinoa,
couscous*

5

softer
vegetables
and fruits
*such as avocado,
strawberries, mango*

SEPARATE
items that might go
soft, such as croutons,
nuts, and seeds, with
parchment paper.

4

proteins
*such as fish,
chicken, eggs,
cheese*

3

heavy grains/
pasta/beans
*such as rice, barley,
soba, cannellini beans,
black beans*

2

hard vegetables
*such as cucumber,
carrot, celery, bell pepper,
beet, cherry tomato,
onion, fennel*

1

dressing

GRAINS AND COOKING PLANS

Grains are a wonderful addition to any healthy salad. They will fill you up for hours, and they have satisfying textures and flavors to boot. All of the grains below should be placed in a saucepan with cold water and brought to a boil, then covered and simmered for the suggested cooking time. Many of these grains benefit from toasting in a dry pan before the water is added.

Storing cooked grains

Once grains are cooked, drain any excess water and store in tightly sealed containers for up to five days. Alternatively, freeze in zip-top bags for up to six months. Uncooked grains should be stored in airtight containers in a cool, dark place for up to six months, or frozen for up to a year.

½ CUP GRAIN	AMOUNT OF WATER	COOKING TIME	GLUTEN-FREE	YIELD
barley (pearl)	1½ cups	25 minutes, covered	no	1¾ cups
brown rice (long grain)	1¼ cups	30 to 35 minutes, covered	yes	1½ cups
buckwheat groats	1 cup	10 minutes, covered	yes	2 cups
bulgur	1 cup	10 minutes, covered	no	1½ cups
farro	1¼ cups	25 minutes, covered	no	1½ cups
Kamut	2 cups	45 to 60 minutes, covered	no	1½ cups
quinoa (red or white)	1 cup	10 minutes, covered; steam 10 minutes off heat	yes	1½ cups
spelt	2 cups	60 to 70 minutes, covered	no	1½ cups
wheat berries	2 cups	60 minutes, covered	no	1¼ cups
wild rice	1½ cups	45 to 55 minutes, covered	yes	1¾ cups

WHAT FRUITS AND VEGETABLES TO BUY

The Environmental Working Group (EWG) annually compiles a list of the fruits and vegetables that contain the highest pesticide loads; these are called the "Dirty Dozen Plus." Each of these items tests higher in pesticide concentrations than other produce, so you should always aim to buy organic.

More recently, EWG created a list of the "Clean Fifteen," or produce that is the least likely to contain pesticide residues and are okay to buy nonorganic. Use this as a guide when you plan your shopping.

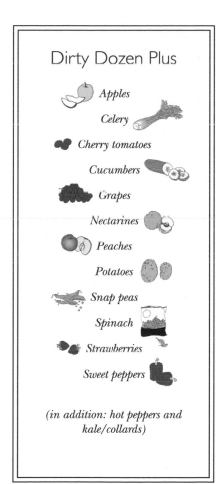

Dirty Dozen Plus

Apples

Celery

Cherry tomatoes

Cucumbers

Grapes

Nectarines

Peaches

Potatoes

Snap peas

Spinach

Strawberries

Sweet peppers

(in addition: hot peppers and kale/collards)

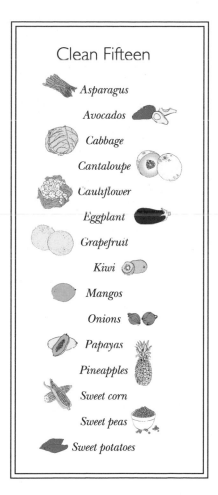

Clean Fifteen

Asparagus

Avocados

Cabbage

Cantaloupe

Cauliflower

Eggplant

Grapefruit

Kiwi

Mangos

Onions

Papayas

Pineapples

Sweet corn

Sweet peas

Sweet potatoes

SALAD DRESSINGS

Salad dressings are like the glue of the salad, harmoniously tying all the other ingredients together. Feel free to mix and match the dressings with the salads, and to add herbs, spices, shallots, or garlic for more intense flavors.

BALSAMIC VINAIGRETTE

Makes: 1 cup — Time: 5 minutes

YOU NEED
⅓ cup balsamic vinegar • 2 teaspoons Dijon mustard
⅔ cup extra-virgin olive oil • Sea salt flakes and freshly ground black pepper

Place the vinegar, mustard, and olive oil in a small jar and season with salt and pepper. Seal the jar and shake vigorously.

LEMON VINAIGRETTE

Makes: ⅔ cup — Time: 5 minutes

YOU NEED

2 teaspoons Dijon mustard • 1 teaspoon lemon zest
3½ tablespoons lemon juice • 7 tablespoons extra-virgin olive oil
1 small clove garlic, very finely chopped
Sea salt flakes and freshly ground black pepper

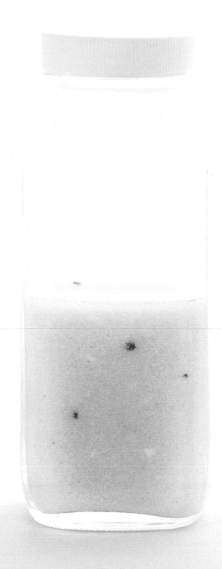

Place the mustard, lemon zest, lemon juice, olive oil, and garlic in a small jar and season with salt and pepper. Seal the jar and shake vigorously.

TAHINI ZINGER

Makes: ½ cup — Time: 10 minutes

YOU NEED
2 tablespoons tahini • 1-ounce piece of ginger, peeled and finely grated

1 clove garlic, finely grated • 2 tablespoons lemon juice

2 teaspoons maple syrup • 1 tablespoon extra-virgin olive oil

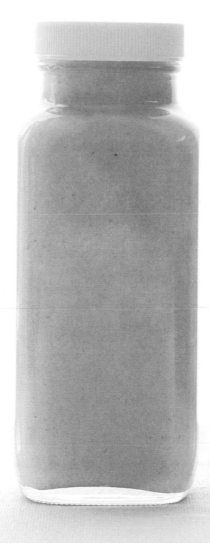

Place the tahini, ginger, garlic, lemon juice, maple syrup, and
olive oil in a small jar. Seal the jar and shake vigorously.

FRENCH VINAIGRETTE

Makes: 1 cup – Time: 5 minutes

YOU NEED

⅓ cup white wine vinegar • 2 teaspoons Dijon mustard
⅔ cup extra-virgin olive oil • 2 tablespoons finely chopped shallot
1 teaspoon chopped tarragon
Sea salt flakes and freshly ground black pepper

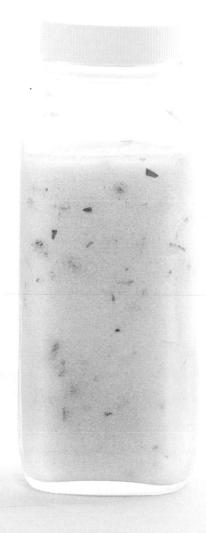

Place the vinegar, mustard, olive oil, shallot, and tarragon in a small jar and season with salt and pepper. Seal the jar and shake vigorously.

THAI PICK-ME-UP

Makes: about 6 tablespoons — Time: 10 minutes

YOU NEED

1-ounce piece of ginger, peeled and finely grated

1 large clove garlic, finely grated • ¼ small red chile, finely grated

1 tablespoon reduced-sodium soy sauce • 2 tablespoons lime juice

1 teaspoon honey • 1 tablespoon vegetable oil • 1 teaspoon fish sauce

Place the ginger, garlic, chile, soy sauce, lime juice, honey, vegetable oil, and fish sauce in a small jar. Seal the jar and shake vigorously.

CAESAR DRESSING

Makes: ⅓ cup — Time: 10 minutes

YOU NEED

2 cloves garlic, finely grated • 1 ounce finely grated Parmesan

1 anchovy, minced • 2 teaspoons Dijon mustard • ½ teaspoon Worcestershire sauce

Zest and juice of 1 lemon • ½ teaspoon coarsely ground black pepper

¼ cup low-fat plain Greek yogurt

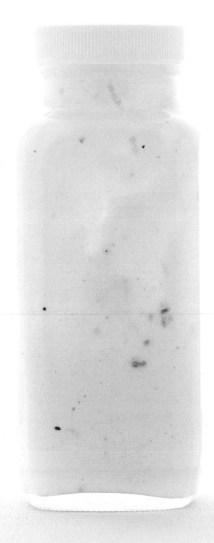

Place the garlic, Parmesan, anchovy, mustard, Worcestershire sauce, lemon zest, lemon juice, pepper, and yogurt in a small jar. Seal the jar and shake vigorously.

GREEN GODDESS

Makes: 1¼ cups — Time: 10 minutes

YOU NEED

1 avocado, peeled and pitted • 1 green onion, coarsely chopped

A small handful of basil leaves • 2 tablespoons lemon juice

6 tablespoons extra-virgin olive oil • 1 tablespoon chopped tarragon

4 tablespoons water

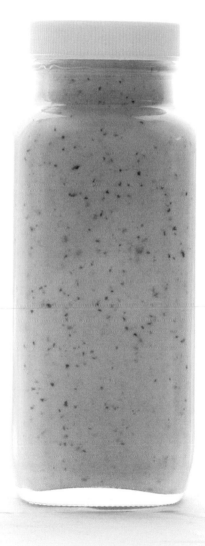

Purée the avocado, green onion, basil, lemon juice, olive oil, tarragon, and water in a blender until very smooth. Store in an airtight container.

RED WINE VINAIGRETTE

Makes: 1 cup — Time: 5 minutes

YOU NEED

2 teaspoons Dijon mustard • ⅓ cup red wine vinegar

⅔ cup extra-virgin olive oil • Sea salt flakes and freshly ground black pepper

Place the mustard, vinegar, and olive oil in a small jar and season with salt and pepper. Seal the jar and shake vigorously.

APPLE CIDER VINAIGRETTE

Makes: 1 cup – Time: 5 minutes

YOU NEED

2 teaspoons whole-grain mustard • ⅓ cup apple cider vinegar

⅔ cup extra-virgin olive oil • Sea salt flakes and freshly ground black pepper

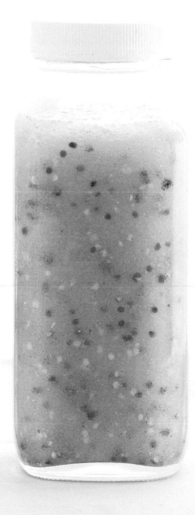

Place the mustard, vinegar, and olive oil in a small jar and season
with salt and pepper. Seal the jar and shake vigorously.

CREAMY DRESSING

Makes: ½ cup – Time: 5 minutes

YOU NEED
3 tablespoons sour cream • 3 tablespoons plain yogurt • 2 tablespoons lemon juice
1 tablespoon chopped chervil • Sea salt flakes and freshly ground black pepper

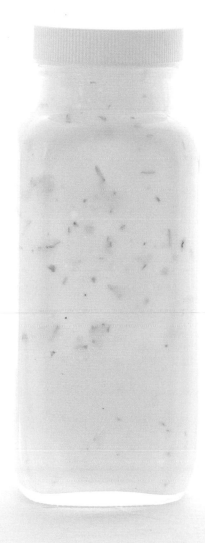

Place the sour cream, yogurt, lemon juice, and chervil in a small jar and season with salt and pepper. Seal the jar and shake vigorously.

ALMOND MISO DRESSING

Makes: ½ cup — Time: 10 minutes

YOU NEED

2 tablespoons creamy almond butter

½-ounce piece of ginger, peeled and finely grated • 1 teaspoon white miso

1 teaspoon maple syrup • 1 teaspoon finely chopped red chile

1 tablespoon lemon juice • 2 tablespoons extra-virgin olive oil

3 tablespoons water

In a small bowl, whisk together the almond butter, ginger, miso, maple syrup, chile, lemon juice, olive oil, and water. Store in an airtight container.

RAW

A raw-food diet promises a wide array of health benefits, from weight loss to lower blood pressure. In this chapter, you will find salads that are raw and vegan while also being nutrient dense, colorful, and delicious. All of the recipes in this chapter are made in pint (2-cup) jars.

KALE, AVOCADO, POMEGRANATE, AND TAHINI

Makes: 1 pint – Time: 10 minutes

YOU NEED

1 to 2 tablespoons Tahini Zinger (page 18)

3 ounces lacinato kale, thick stems removed and leaves finely sliced

½ small avocado, peeled, pitted, and chopped

A small handful of mixed sprouts (such as broccoli, chickpea, lentil, alfalfa, radish)

A small handful of pomegranate seeds

1 tablespoon mixed seeds (such as pumpkin and sunflower)

This salad is full of antioxidants, heart-healthy fats, and potassium.

(A) *Antioxidant* (BPL) *Blood Pressure Lowering* (M) *Mineral Rich*

Place the dressing in the bottom of a pint jar. Add half of the kale.
Top with the avocado, then the remaining kale, then the sprouts, then the
pomegranate seeds and mixed seeds. Seal the jar tightly. Once the salad
has been shaken together, leave for 10 minutes to soften the kale.

VEGGIE DRAW

Makes: 1 pint — Time: 10 minutes

YOU NEED
1 to 2 tablespoons Almond Miso Dressing (page 34)

1 ounce very finely sliced fennel • 1¾ ounces cherry tomatoes, halved

1½ ounces seedless cucumber, halved and very finely sliced

1 small carrot, peeled and very finely sliced • ⅓ cup frozen corn, thawed

½ small avocado, peeled, pitted, and sliced

This salad is a great detoxifier and immunity booster.

DX *Detoxifying* **I** *Immune Boosting* **G** *Gluten-Free*

Place the dressing in the bottom of a pint jar. Add the fennel, then the tomatoes, followed by the cucumber, carrot, and corn, and, finally, the avocado (if eating the same day). Seal the jar tightly.

RADISH, CARROT, AND BABY KALE

Makes: 1 pint – Time: 10 minutes

YOU NEED

1 to 2 tablespoons Green Goddess (page 26)

2 large radishes, very thinly sliced

2 small carrots, peeled and coarsely grated • 2½ tablespoons raisins

2 green onions, very thinly sliced • A handful of baby kale

This salad is great for skin, eyesight, and digestion, and for preventing infection.

SC *Skin Cleansing* **D** *Digestion Boosting* **I** *Immune Boosting*

Place the dressing in the bottom of a pint jar. Add the radishes, then the carrots, then the raisins, green onions, and baby kale. Seal the jar tightly.

CRUNCHY CABBAGE

Makes: 1 pint — Time: 10 minutes

YOU NEED
1 to 2 tablespoons Apple Cider Vinaigrette (page 30)
2 thin green onions, finely sliced • 3 ounces red cabbage, chopped
1 celery stalk, chopped • ½ red or orange bell pepper, seeded and sliced
1 large radish, finely sliced

This salad is an excellent source of vitamin C, which revs up your immune system and keeps your skin youthful.

HD *Hydrating* **I** *Immune Boosting* **SR** *Skin Repairing*

Place the vinaigrette in the bottom of a pint jar. Add the green onions, then the cabbage, then the celery, bell pepper, and radish. Seal the jar tightly.

TOPSY-TURVY

Makes: 1 pint – Time: 10 minutes

YOU NEED

1 to 2 tablespoons extra-virgin olive oil • 2 green onions, finely chopped

1¾ ounces cherry tomatoes, halved • 6 ounces turnip, coarsely grated (not peeled)

½ yellow bell pepper, seeded and chopped • 2 ounces Persian cucumber, chopped

This is a great salad for keeping your digestive system healthy.

D *Digestion Boosting* **I** *Immune Boosting* **DX** *Detoxifying*

Place the olive oil in the bottom of a pint jar. Add the green onions, then the tomatoes, followed by the turnip, bell pepper, and, finally, the cucumber. Seal the jar tightly.

SOUTHEAST ASIAN

Makes: 1 pint — Time: 5 minutes

YOU NEED

1 to 2 tablespoons Thai Pick-Me-Up (page 22)

1 small carrot, peeled and julienned • 1 ounce enoki mushrooms

2½ ounces chopped baby bok choy • ¾ ounce cashew nuts

This salad is full of vitamin A, which is essential for vision, the immune system, and reproduction.

 *Antioxidant*  *Infection fighting*  *Fertility Supporting*

Place the dressing in the bottom of a pint jar. Add the carrot, followed by the mushrooms, baby bok choy, and, finally, the cashews (separated by parchment if not eating that day). Seal the jar tightly.

SQUASH AND LEMON

Makes: 1 pint — Time: 5 minutes

YOU NEED

1 teaspoon lemon zest • 1 tablespoon lemon juice

1 tablespoon extra-virgin olive oil • Sea salt flakes and freshly ground black pepper

5 ounces mixed summer squash (such as zucchini, yellow squash, patty pan),

thinly sliced • ½ ounce mixed microgreens (such as arugula or kale)

This cleansing salad is great for purifying the blood and flushing out toxins.

HD *Hydrating* **DX** *Detoxifying* **CL** *Cleansing*

Place the lemon zest, lemon juice, and olive oil in a pint jar, with a pinch
each of salt and pepper. Add the squash and swirl the jar to coat
in the oil. Top with the microgreens. Seal the jar tightly.

SMALL JARS

In this chapter you will find salads perfect for a lighter lunch or to serve as an accompaniment to a larger meal— small in size, but filling nonetheless. To turn these into bigger meals, simply double the ingredients and use quart jars. Remember to use parchment paper to separate any ingredients that might go soft, such as croutons and nuts.

SUPER GREEN SALAD

Makes: 1 pint — Time: 5 minutes

YOU NEED

1 to 2 tablespoons Apple Cider Vinaigrette (page 30)

1 ounce broccoli, finely shaved

1 ounce asparagus, thick stems discarded, finely shaved

⅓ ounce baby spinach leaves • 2 teaspoons hemp hearts

The hemp hearts in this salad are full of essential fatty acids, calcium, and iron, and their high protein content helps to control blood sugar levels.

D *Digestion Boosting* **SB** *Stamina Boosting* **BS** *Blood Sugar Stabilizing*

Place the vinaigrette in the bottom of a pint jar. Add the broccoli, followed by the asparagus and spinach and, finally, the hemp hearts. Seal the jar tightly.

FIGS AND BLUE CHEESE

Makes: 1 pint — Time: 5 minutes

YOU NEED

1 to 2 tablespoons Balsamic Vinaigrette (page 14) • 1 small shallot, finely sliced

2 fresh or dried figs, stems removed, thickly sliced

1 ounce blue cheese, crumbled • ¾ ounce walnuts, coarsely chopped

⅓ ounce frisée

The figs are a great source of fiber to help with weight management, potassium to control blood pressure, and calcium, a mineral essential for your bones.

 *Weight Managing*  *Hunger Suppressing*  *Blood Sugar Stabilizing*

Place the vinaigrette in the bottom of a pint jar. Add the shallot, then the figs, followed by the blue cheese and the walnuts (if eating that day), and, finally, the frisée. Seal the jar tightly.

SPROUTS, PARMESAN, AND PECANS

Makes: 1 pint — Time: 10 minutes

YOU NEED

1 to 2 tablespoons Lemon Vinaigrette (page 16) • 3½ ounces brussels sprouts,
trimmed and shredded • 1 ounce Parmesan cheese, shaved
2 tablespoons dried cranberries • 3 tablespoons toasted pecans, chopped

The brussels sprouts in this salad are full of antioxidants, immune-boosting vitamin C, and anti-inflammatory vitamin K, and are known for reducing cholesterol.

 *Bone Strengthening* **CR** *Cholesterol Reducing* **V** *Vitamin Enhancing*

Place the vinaigrette in the bottom of a pint jar. Add the brussels sprouts, followed by the Parmesan, then the cranberries, and, finally, the pecans. Seal the jar tightly.

GREENS, FETA, BLUEBERRIES, AND WALNUTS

Makes: 1 pint — Time: 5 minutes

YOU NEED

1 to 2 tablespoons French Vinaigrette (page 20) • 1 ounce feta cheese, broken into
small pieces • A pinch of red pepper flakes • 1½ ounces blueberries
¾ ounce toasted walnuts, chopped • ½ ounce mizuna • ½ ounce baby kale

This salad is full of antioxidants that boost heart health, repair cells, and reduce the risk of cancer.

I *Immune Boosting* **BR** *Blood Regulating* **BS** *Blood Sugar Stabilizing*

Place the vinaigrette in the bottom of a pint jar. Add the feta, red pepper flakes, and blueberries, then the walnuts, mizuna, and baby kale. Seal the jar tightly.

CELERY AND PARMESAN

Makes: 1 pint — Time: 5 minutes

YOU NEED

1 to 2 tablespoons Lemon Vinaigrette (page 16) • 3½ ounces celery, sliced
½ cup cooked or canned chickpeas • 1 ounce raisins
A small handful of celery leaves • A small handful of roasted, unsalted almonds,
chopped • ¾ ounce Parmesan cheese, broken into small pieces

The chickpeas in this salad are a terrific source of protein and fiber, which will keep you full. They also contain exceptional levels of iron, vitamin B-6, and magnesium.

HD *Hydrating* **BE** *Blood Enhancing* **HS** *Hunger Suppressing*

Place the vinaigrette in the bottom of a pint jar. Add the sliced celery, followed by the chickpeas, raisins, and celery leaves. Last, add the almonds and Parmesan. Seal the jar tightly.

LEMON SUMMER SQUASH NOODLES

Makes: 1 pint — Time: 10 minutes

YOU NEED
1 to 2 tablespoons Lemon Vinaigrette (page 16)

3½ ounces green and yellow summer squash, cut into noodles • 1 ounce feta cheese

¼ ounce basil leaves • ¼ ounce chopped chives • 1 tablespoon toasted pine nuts

Full of heart-friendly monounsaturated fatty acids, this salad helps reduce cholesterol levels; the volatile oils help protect against unwanted bacterial growth.

HD *Hydrating* **BR** *Blood Regulating* **W** *Weight Managing*

Place the vinaigrette in the bottom of a pint jar. Add the squash noodles, followed by the feta, basil, and chives, and, finally, the pine nuts. Seal the jar tightly.

ARUGULA, FENNEL, AND PARMESAN

Makes: 1 pint — Time: 10 minutes

YOU NEED

1 to 2 tablespoons Lemon Vinaigrette (page 16) • 2½ ounces fennel, thinly sliced

1 ounce baby arugula • ½ small avocado, peeled, pitted, and sliced

¾ ounce Parmesan cheese, shaved

This salad is a terrific source of potassium, a mineral
that helps lower blood pressure.

W *Weight Managing* **D** *Digestion Boosting* **G** *Gluten-Free*

Place the vinaigrette in the bottom of a pint jar. Add the fennel, followed by the
arugula, then the avocado. Cut a small square of parchment paper, place directly
on top of the avocado, and add the Parmesan. Seal the jar tightly.

CELERY ROOT AND BEET REMOULADE

Makes: 1 pint — Time: 15 minutes

YOU NEED

1 to 2 tablespoons Creamy Dressing (page 32, made with 1 tablespoon whole-grain
mustard and flat-leaf parsley) • 1¾ ounces celery root, peeled and julienned
1¾ ounces mixed colored beets, peeled and julienned
1 smoked mackerel fillet, skinned and flaked • 1 teaspoon poppy seeds

This salad is full of nitrates that help lower blood pressure and fight heart disease, and essential fatty acids for cell growth and repair.

AP *Aphrodisiac* **BR** *Blood Regulating* **LC** *Liver Cleansing*

Place the dressing in the bottom of a pint jar. Add the celery root, followed by the beets, then the mackerel and poppy seeds. Seal the jar tightly.

BROCCOLI RABE, KALE, AND KAMUT

Makes: 1 pint – Time: 25 minutes

YOU NEED

1 to 2 tablespoons Tahini Zinger (page 18) • 1 small shallot, sliced

⅓ cup cooked seasoned Kamut • 4½ ounces broccoli rabe, trimmed and blanched

3½ ounces kale, stems removed and leaves blanched

1 tablespoon toasted pumpkin seeds • 1 tablespoon toasted shelled pistachios

This is full of vitamins A and C, both of which fight off dangerous free radicals that can cause damage to your body's cells.

ME *Mineral Enhancing*   **BS** *Blood Sugar Stabilizing*   **N** *Nervous System Supporting*

Place the dressing in the bottom of a pint jar. Add the shallot, followed by the Kamut. Squeeze any excess water out of the broccoli rabe and kale, coarsely chop, and add to the jar. Add the pumpkin seeds and pistachios. Seal the jar tightly.

BLACK BEAN AND CORN

Makes: 1 pint — Time: 5 minutes

YOU NEED

3 tablespoons fresh tomato salsa • ⅓ cup fresh or frozen corn

⅓ cup cooked or canned black beans

½ small avocado, peeled, pitted, and diced

¾ ounce romaine lettuce, chopped • A small handful of tortilla strips

The black beans in this salad provide wonderful support to the digestive tract, lowering the risk for colon cancer.

F *Filling* **D** *Digestion Boosting* **CR** *Cholesterol Reducing*

Place the salsa in the bottom of a pint jar. Add the corn, followed by the black beans, then the avocado and romaine. Cut a small square of parchment paper, place directly on top of the romaine, and add the tortilla strips. Seal the jar tightly.

WATERMELON, TOMATO, AND FETA

Makes: 1 pint — Time: 10 minutes

YOU NEED
1 to 2 tablespoons Red Wine Vinaigrette (page 28)

¼ small red onion, thinly sliced • 2½ ounces yellow cherry tomatoes, halved

3 ounces peeled seedless watermelon, cut into small cubes • 1 ounce feta cheese

⅓ ounce basil • ⅓ ounce parsley leaves

This salad is full of beneficial nutrients and antioxidants; it is a rich source of vitamins A and C and folic acid.

H *Hydrating* D *Digestion Boosting* N *Nervous System Supporting*

Place the vinaigrette in the bottom of a pint jar. Add the red onion, then the cherry tomatoes, followed by the watermelon, feta, basil, and parsley. Seal the jar tightly.

LIMA BEAN, POMEGRANATE, AND PESTO

Makes: 1 pint — Time: 10 minutes

YOU NEED

2 tablespoons pesto • ½ cup cooked or canned baby lima beans

¼ cup pomegranate seeds • 1½ ounces celery, sliced

1 ounce arugula, coarsely chopped • 1 tablespoon toasted pine nuts

The pomegranate seeds in this salad contain high levels of flavonoids and polyphenols, powerful antioxidants that offer protection against heart disease and cancer.

BR *Blood Regulating*　**I** *Immune Boosting*　**BPL** *Blood Pressure Lowering*

Place the pesto in the bottom of a pint jar. Add the lima beans, followed by the pomegranate seeds, then the celery and arugula. Add the pine nuts. Seal the jar tightly.

GRILLED PEPPER, BEANS, AND GOAT CHEESE

Makes: 1 pint — Time: 10 minutes

YOU NEED
1 to 2 tablespoons French Vinaigrette (page 20)
1 small yellow bell pepper, cored, seeded, quartered, and grilled
3 tablespoons cooked or canned cranberry beans • 1¾ ounces green beans,
trimmed, grilled, and halved • ¾ ounce goat cheese • A small handful of tarragon
leaves, coarsely chopped • 2¼ ounces Belgian endive, chopped

This is full of carotenoids, antioxidants that can help prevent some forms of cancer and heart disease and enhance your immune response to infections.

G *Gluten-Free* **IF** *Infection Fighting* **CS** *Cardiovascular Supporting*

Place the vinaigrette in the bottom of a pint jar. Add the grilled bell pepper, followed by the cranberry beans, then the grilled green beans, goat cheese, tarragon, and, finally, the endive. Seal the jar tightly.

STRAWBERRY, POPPY SEED, AND HALLOUMI

Makes: 1 pint — Time: 15 minutes

YOU NEED

2 tablespoons Balsamic Vinaigrette (page 14) • 1¾ ounces fennel, thinly sliced
2½ ounces strawberries, hulled and sliced • 1 ounce watercress • 1 teaspoon
poppy seeds • 1¾ ounces halloumi cheese, grilled or lightly seared

This salad is a great source of vitamin C for the immune system; nitrates, which lower blood pressure; and vitamin K for bone health.

(G) *Gluten-Free* (AI) *Anti-inflammatory* (B) *Blood Stimulating*

Place the vinaigrette in the bottom of a pint jar. Add the fennel, then the strawberries, followed by the watercress and poppy seeds. Cut a small square of parchment paper, place directly on top of the watercress, and add the halloumi. Seal the jar tightly.

SMOKED SALMON, CAPERS, AND WATERCRESS

Makes: 1 pint — Time: 10 minutes

YOU NEED
1 to 2 tablespoons Apple Cider Vinaigrette (page 30)

¼ small red onion, thinly sliced • ½ tablespoon capers, rinsed

1¾ ounces Persian cucumber, sliced • 1¾ ounces smoked salmon

¼ small avocado, peeled, pitted, and sliced

A small handful of flat-leaf parsley leaves • ⅓ ounce watercress

This salad is high in heart-healthy fats, which help provide protection from high cholesterol, diabetes, and high blood pressure.

(G) *Gluten-Free* (HS) *Hunger Suppressing* (CR) *Cholesterol Reducing*

Place the vinaigrette in the bottom of a pint jar. Add the red onion, followed by the capers, then the cucumber, smoked salmon, avocado, parsley, and, finally, the watercress. Seal the jar tightly.

GRAPEFRUIT, PISTACHIO, AND WATERCRESS

Makes: 1 pint — Time: 10 minutes

YOU NEED
1 to 2 tablespoons Thai Pick-Me-Up (page 22)

1 green onion, finely sliced • 3 ounces segmented grapefruit

1 ounce radish, very thinly sliced • ¾ ounce watercress • 2 tablespoons pistachios

This is a great weight-loss salad, with lots of fiber to keep you full and water to keep you hydrated.

 *Hydrating*  *Detoxifying*  *Gluten-Free*

Place the dressing in the bottom of a pint jar. Add the green onion, followed by the grapefruit, then the radish, watercress, and pistachios. Seal the jar tightly.

VERY ASPARAGUS

Makes: 1 pint — Time: 15 minutes

YOU NEED

2 tablespoons Red Wine Vinaigrette (page 28)

1 green onion, thinly sliced • 1 large radish, thinly sliced

7 ounces asparagus, trimmed, grilled, and chopped • 1 tablespoon capers, drained

1 hard-boiled egg, chopped • ¾ ounce kale microgreens

The asparagus contains anti-inflammatory micronutrients and antioxidants, which reduce the risk of common chronic health problems such as heart disease.

HD *Hydrating* **HS** *Hunger Suppressing* **G** *Gluten-Free*

Place the vinaigrette in the bottom of a pint jar. Add the green onion, followed by the radish, grilled asparagus, then the capers, egg, and, finally, the microgreens. Seal the jar tightly.

TABBOULEH

Makes: 1 pint — Time: 10 minutes

YOU NEED
1 to 2 tablespoons Lemon Vinaigrette (page 16) • 2 green onions, very thinly sliced

⅓ cup cooked and seasoned bulgur • 1¾ ounces tomatoes, chopped

1¾ ounces Persian cucumber, chopped • ¼ ounce small mint leaves

¼ ounce small flat-leaf parsley leaves

This is high in fiber and low in glycemic load, which keeps your blood sugar stable.

HD *Hydrating*　**D** *Digestion Boosting*　**BS** *Blood Sugar Stabilizing*

Place the vinaigrette in the bottom of a pint jar. Add the green
onions, followed by the bulgur, then the tomatoes, cucumber,
mint, and parsley leaves. Seal the jar tightly.

TOMATO, MOZZARELLA, AND ARUGULA

Makes: 1 pint — Time: 5 minutes

YOU NEED

1 to 2 tablespoons Balsamic Vinaigrette (page 14)

¼ small red onion, finely sliced • 3 large cherry tomatoes, halved

1¾ ounces marinated bocconcini, halved

¼ small avocado, peeled, pitted, and chopped • ¾ ounce baby arugula

The cherry tomatoes in this salad are full of the antioxidant lycopene, which can reduce your risk of cardiovascular disease and cancers.

 Gluten-Free *BF* Bacteria Fighting *N* Nervous System Supporting

Place the vinaigrette in the bottom of a pint jar. Add the red onion, followed by the tomatoes, bocconcini, avocado, and, finally, the baby arugula. Seal the jar tightly.

WHEAT BERRY, APPLE, AND DATE

Makes: 1 pint — Time: 10 minutes

YOU NEED

1 to 2 tablespoons Almond Miso Dressing (page 34) • 1¾ ounces Granny Smith
or other tart apple, sliced • ⅓ cup cooked wheat berries
5 small, soft pitted dates, chopped • ⅓ ounce microgreens (such as
kale, arugula, or sunflower) • A small handful of crunchy sprouts
(such as adzuki, chickpea, or lentil)

The sprouted grains, beans, and seeds in this salad are higher in protein, fiber, vitamins, and essential fatty acids than their unsprouted counterparts.

D *Digestion Boosting* **HS** *Hunger Suppressing* **BO** *Bone Strengthening*

Place the dressing in the bottom of a pint jar. Add the apple, followed by the wheat berries, dates, microgreens, and, finally, the sprouts. Seal the jar tightly.

TUNA, FENNEL, AND WHITE BEAN

Makes: 1 pint – Time: 10 minutes

YOU NEED

2 tablespoons Lemon Vinaigrette (page 16) • 1¾ ounces finely shaved fennel

⅓ cup cooked or canned chickpeas • 1 green onion, finely sliced

1¾ ounces drained good-quality tuna • 1 ounce pitted Kalamata olives, chopped

¾ ounce alfalfa, radish, or broccoli sprouts

This salad is high in fiber and protein with a low glycemic index.

I *Immune Boosting* **ME** *Mineral Enhancing* **G** *Gluten-Free*

Place the vinaigrette in the bottom of a pint jar. Add the fennel,
followed by the chickpeas, then the green onion, tuna, olives,
and, finally, the sprouts. Seal the jar tightly.

BIG JARS

These salads are a complete meal, including grains, lean proteins, and lots of fruits and vegetables. They are hearty but healthy. Think of the grains and greens as merely suggestions that you can mix and match based on what you have available. Remember to add fruit on the day you plan to eat the salad to prevent undesirable sogginess!

CHICKEN AND KALE CAESAR

Makes: 1 quart — Time: 10 minutes

YOU NEED

2 to 3 tablespoons Caesar Dressing (page 24) • 4 ounces cherry tomatoes, halved

2¼ ounces cooked chicken breast, chopped

1¾ ounces chopped curly kale • ½ ounce shredded Parmesan cheese

A small handful of croutons

This is packed with folate, a B vitamin essential for brain development.

DX *Detoxifying* **HS** *Hunger Suppressing* **N** *Nervous System Supporting*

Place the dressing in the bottom of a quart jar. Add the cherry tomatoes, followed by the chicken, kale, and Parmesan. Cut a small square of parchment paper, place directly on top of the Parmesan, and add the croutons. Seal the jar tightly.

NIÇOISE AND BUCKWHEAT

Makes: 1 quart — Time: 15 minutes

YOU NEED
2 to 3 tablespoons French Vinaigrette (page 20)

3 ounces Campari tomatoes, chopped • ⅔ cup cooked and seasoned buckwheat

1¾ ounces green beans, trimmed, blanched, and cut into thirds

1 hard-boiled egg, chopped • 1¾ ounces drained and flaked tuna

1½ ounces Niçoise olives • 1 ounce mesclun mix

This salad is full of protein and fiber to keep you fuller for longer.

D *Digestion Boosting* **HS** *Hunger Suppressing* **I** *Immune Boosting*

Place the vinaigrette in the bottom of a quart jar. Add the tomatoes, then the buckwheat, green beans, egg, tuna, olives, and, finally, the mesclun mix. Seal the jar tightly.

SMOKED SALMON, QUINOA, AND TZATZIKI

Makes: 1 quart — Time: 10 minutes

YOU NEED

¼ cup tzatziki • 1¾ ounces celery, very thinly sliced

2 small multicolored beets, peeled and very thinly sliced

½ cup cooked and seasoned white and red quinoa

1¾ cups hot-smoked flaked salmon • 1 ounce beet greens, chopped

2 tablespoons chopped toasted hazelnuts

The beet greens contain more iron than spinach and may help fight Alzheimer's disease and osteoporosis.

 *Skin Repairing* **BF** *Bacteria Fighting* **G** *Gluten-Free*

Place the tzatziki in the bottom of a quart jar. Add the celery, followed by the beets, then the quinoa, flaked salmon, beet greens, and, finally, the hazelnuts. Seal the jar tightly.

FATTOUSH

Makes: 1 quart — Time: 10 minutes

YOU NEED
2 to 3 tablespoons Lemon Vinaigrette (page 16) • 3 ounces cherry tomatoes, halved

1¾ ounces pitted Kalamata olives, halved

3 ounces Persian cucumber, chopped • ¼ ounce mint leaves

¼ ounce flat-leaf parsley leaves • 2 ounces romaine lettuce, chopped

A small handful of pita chips

This is a great salad for digestion and flushing out toxins.

 *Hydrating* **DX** *Detoxifying* **CL** *Cleansing*

Place the vinaigrette in the bottom of a quart jar. Add the cherry tomatoes,
followed by the olives, cucumber, mint, parsley, and romaine lettuce.
Cut a small square of parchment paper, place directly on top of the romaine,
and add the pita chips. Seal the jar tightly.

COBB SALAD

Makes: 1 quart — Time: 15 minutes

YOU NEED

2 to 3 tablespoons Red Wine Vinaigrette (page 28) • 2½ ounces tomato, chopped
2½ ounces Persian cucumber, chopped • 2 ounces cooked chicken breast,
shredded • 1 large hard-boiled egg, chopped • ½ small avocado, peeled,
pitted, and chopped • 1 ounce crumbled blue cheese (such as Gorgonzola)
1¾ ounces romaine lettuce, chopped

This is a superlean protein booster. Not only does protein fill you up, it helps build and repair tissues and is a building block for bones, muscle, skin, and blood.

GF *Gluten-Free*   **HS** *Hunger Suppressing*   **MO** *Mood Enhancing*

Place the vinaigrette in the bottom of a quart jar. Add the tomato, followed by the cucumber, then the chicken, egg, avocado, blue cheese, and, finally, the romaine lettuce. Seal the jar tightly.

ASIAN CHICKEN

Makes: 1 quart — Time: 15 minutes

YOU NEED

2 to 3 tablespoons Thai Pick-Me-Up (page 22)

2 green onions, finely sliced • 2½ ounces mixed shredded carrot and celery

1 ounce soba noodles, cooked and cooled

½ red chile (such as red jalapeño), very thinly sliced

1¾ ounces cooked, skinless chicken breast, shredded

3 tablespoons chopped roasted unsalted peanuts • ¼ ounce cilantro leaves

The capsaicin in red chiles fights inflammation, has cardiovascular benefits, is a natural pain reliever, and will help clear nasal congestion.

IF *Infection Fighting* **BE** *Blood Enhancng* **AI** *Anti-inflammatory*

Place the dressing in the bottom of a quart jar. Add the green onions, followed by the shredded carrot and celery, cooked soba noodles, red chile, chicken, peanuts, and, finally, the cilantro leaves. Seal the jar tightly.

CURRIED CHICKEN

Makes: 1 quart — Time: 15 minutes

YOU NEED

2 to 3 tablespoons Creamy Dressing (page 32, mixed with 1 teaspoon
mango chutney and ½ teaspoon curry powder) • 1 celery stalk, chopped
½ cup cooked and seasoned brown rice • 2½ ounces cooked, skinless chicken
breast, shredded • ¾ ounce red leaf lettuce, torn • ⅓ ounce cilantro leaves
A small handful of almonds

This is a good source of manganese, which helps the body process cholesterol, proteins, and carbohydrates.

HD *Hydrating* **D** *Digestion Boosting* **G** *Gluten-Free*

Place the dressing in the bottom of a quart jar. Add the celery, followed by the brown rice, then the chicken, lettuce, cilantro leaves, and, finally, the almonds. Seal the jar tightly.

LENTILS WITH EGGPLANT AND RAISINS

Makes: 1 quart – Time: 5 minutes

YOU NEED

2 tablespoons Red Wine Vinaigrette (page 28) • 1 cup cooked Puy lentils

1¾ ounces marinated artichokes • 5 ounces marinated eggplant slices

1 ounce goat cheese, thickly sliced • 2 tablespoons golden raisins

1¾ ounces grilled radicchio, chopped

The eggplant in this salad is rich in the antioxidant nasunin, which protects the essential fats in brain cell membranes.

Place the vinaigrette in the bottom of a quart jar. Add the lentils and stir to combine. Add the artichokes, followed by the eggplant, then the goat cheese, raisins, and, finally, the radicchio. Seal the jar tightly.

FALAFEL SALAD

Makes: 1 quart — Time: 10 minutes

YOU NEED

2 to 3 tablespoons Tahini Zinger (page 18) • ½ small red onion, chopped

3½ ounces red cabbage, chopped • 1 pickle, chopped

½ cup cooked or canned chickpeas • 2½ ounces falafel,

broken into chunks • 2½ ounces romaine lettuce, chopped

This salad helps keep your blood sugar stable and keeps hunger at bay.

HD *Hydrating*　**A** *Antioxidant*　**LC** *Liver Cleansing*

Place the dressing in the bottom of a quart jar. Add the onion, followed by the red cabbage, then the pickle, chickpeas, falafel, and, finally, the romaine lettuce. Seal the jar tightly.

WILD RICE AND NECTARINE

Makes: 1 quart — Time: 10 minutes

YOU NEED

2 to 3 tablespoons Balsamic Vinaigrette (page 14)

3 ounces sugar snap peas, trimmed and cut into thirds

⅔ cup cooked and seasoned wild rice • 1 small nectarine, pitted and chopped

1 ounce blue cheese • 1 ounce baby arugula

The wild rice in this salad contains twice as much protein as brown rice and has 30 times the antioxidants of white rice.

AZ *Alkalizing* **D** *Digestion Boosting* **G** *Gluten-Free*

Place the vinaigrette in the bottom of a quart jar. Add the sugar snap peas, followed by the wild rice, then the nectarine, blue cheese, and, finally, the arugula. Seal the jar tightly.

FARRO WITH GRAPES AND LIMA BEANS

Makes: 1 quart — Time: 15 minutes

YOU NEED

2 tablespoons Balsamic Vinaigrette (page 14)

½ yellow bell pepper, seeded and sliced • ½ cup cooked and seasoned farro

3½ ounces seedless red and green grapes, halved • ⅔ cup cooked or canned baby
lima beans • 4½ ounces Swiss chard, stems removed and leaves
coarsely chopped • 1 ounce extra-mature or applewood-smoked Cheddar,
cut into small cubes • 3 tablespoons chopped toasted hazelnuts

This salad is full of phytonutrients that help regulate blood sugar, and also calcium, magnesium, and vitamin K for bone support.

D *Digestion Boosting* **BO** *Bone Strengthening* **BPL** *Blood Pressure Lowering*

Place the vinaigrette in the bottom of a quart jar. Add the bell pepper, followed by the farro, then the grapes, lima beans, Swiss chard, Cheddar, and, finally, the hazelnuts. Seal the jar tightly.

PEACH, QUINOA, AND DANDELION

Makes: 1 quart — Time: 10 minutes

YOU NEED

2 tablespoons Lemon Vinaigrette (page 16, with 1 teaspoon honey added)

⅔ cup cooked or canned chickpeas • 1 large peach, peeled, pitted, and chopped

¾ cup cooked and seasoned quinoa • 1¾ ounces dandelion, chopped

3 tablespoons chopped toasted almonds

The dandelion helps the liver and gallbladder by regulating bile production. Excess bile entering the bloodstream can wreak havoc on the metabolism.

H *Healing* **LC** *Liver Cleansing* **IF** *Infection Fighting*

Place the vinaigrette in the bottom of a quart jar. Add the chickpeas, followed by the peach and quinoa, then the dandelion, and almonds. Seal the jar tightly.

SALMON AND SPELT

Makes: 1 quart — Time: 10 minutes

YOU NEED
2 to 3 tablespoons Green Goddess (page 26)

3 ounces multicolored cherry tomatoes, halved • ½ cup cooked and seasoned spelt

1 ounce yellow bell pepper, sliced • 2½ ounces cooked skinless salmon, flaked

¾ ounce mizuna • ¾ ounce arugula

The spelt is high in dietary fiber, which helps move food through the digestive tract, speeding up the absorption of nutrients and reducing gastrointestinal complaints.

S *Strengthening* **E** *Energizing* **D** *Digestion Boosting*

Place the dressing in the bottom of a quart jar. Add the tomatoes and spelt, followed by the bell pepper, salmon, and, finally, the mizuna and arugula. Seal the jar tightly.

SUMMER GRILL

Makes: 1 quart — Time: 20 minutes

YOU NEED

2 tablespoons pesto • 1 small yellow squash,
sliced thickly lengthwise and grilled • 8 medium asparagus, trimmed and grilled
⅓ cup cooked or canned white beans • 1 small orange bell pepper, seeded, quartered,
and grilled • 4 collard leaves, thick stems discarded, grilled
¾ ounce ricotta salata, shaved

This salad is packed with vitamins A and C and iron,
which are all essential for healthy skin and hair.

SR *Skin Repairing* **DX** *Detoxifying* **CR** *Cholesterol Reducing*

Place the pesto in the bottom of a quart jar. Chop the squash and add
to the jar. Chop the asparagus and add to the jar. Add the white beans. Chop
the bell pepper and add to the jar. Chop the collards and add to the jar.
Finally, add the ricotta salata. Seal the jar tightly.

PINTO BEAN, BROCCOLI, AND ESCAROLE

Makes: 1 quart — Time: 10 minutes

YOU NEED

2 tablespoons Red Wine Vinaigrette (page 28)

1 small shallot, chopped • ⅔ cup pinto beans mixed with fresh dill

3½ ounces broccoli, chopped • 1¾ ounces feta cheese

1¾ ounces escarole

This salad is rich in vitamin K, which is essential for proper blood clotting, and vitamin C for cold fighting.

I *Immune Boosting*　**D** *Digestion Boosting*　**BS** *Blood Sugar Stabilizing*

Place the vinaigrette in the bottom of a quart jar. Add the shallot, followed by the pinto beans, then the broccoli, feta, and, finally, the escarole. Seal the jar tightly.

KALE, SWEET POTATO, AND BARLEY

Makes: 1 quart – Time: 30 minutes

YOU NEED
2 to 4 tablespoons Apple Cider Vinaigrette (page 30)

½ small red onion, chopped • ¾ cup cooked and seasoned pearl barley

3½ ounces peeled, cubed, and roasted sweet potato

3 ounces cherry tomatoes, halved • 5 ounces curly kale, stems removed,

leaves steamed and chopped • 1 tablespoon toasted pine nuts

This contains the nutrient choline, which helps with sleep, muscle movement, learning, and memory. It helps fat absorption and nerve impulse transmissions.

RJ *Rejuvenating* *CR* *Cholesterol Reducing* *BS* *Blood Sugar Stabilizing*

Place the vinaigrette in the bottom of a quart jar. Add the red onion, followed by the barley, then the sweet potato, tomatoes, steamed kale, and, finally, the pine nuts. Seal the jar tightly.

WALDORF

Makes: 1 quart — Time: 10 minutes

YOU NEED
2 tablespoons Creamy Dressing (page 32)

5 ounces cored and chopped tart apple • 3½ ounces red cabbage, chopped

4½ ounces celery, finely sliced • 1¾ ounces peanuts

This salad is packed with fiber to help keep you regular as well as cleansing your colon and keeping you fuller for longer.

 *Hydrating* **D** *Digestion Boosting* **BPL** *Blood Pressure Lowering*

Place the dressing in the bottom of a quart jar. Add the apple, followed by the red cabbage, celery, and, finally, the peanuts. Seal the jar tightly.

PEA, FAVA BEAN, AND KAMUT

Makes: 1 quart — Time: 15 minutes

YOU NEED

2 to 3 tablespoons Lemon Vinaigrette (page 16, with ⅓ ounce grated Parmesan cheese added) • 2 green onions, finely chopped

½ cup cooked and seasoned Kamut • 3½ ounces fava beans, shelled and blanched

2½ ounces fresh or frozen English peas, blanched

¾ ounce chopped toasted almonds • 1 ounce pea shoots

This is a great salad for weight management—high in dietary fiber, protein, and heart-healthy fats.

D *Digestion Boosting* **B** *Blood Stimulating* **IF** *Infection Fighting*

Place the vinaigrette in the bottom of a quart jar. Add the green onions, followed by the Kamut, fava beans, peas, almonds, and, finally, the pea shoots. Seal the jar tightly.

SWEET-AND-SOUR BUTTERNUT SQUASH

Makes: 1 quart — Time: 30 minutes

YOU NEED
2 tablespoons Thai Pick-Me-Up (page 22)

2 green onions, chopped • ⅔ cup cooked and seasoned brown rice

1¾ ounces carrot, peeled and julienned • 6 ounces peeled, seeded, cubed butternut

squash, roasted • 3½ ounces peeled, pitted, and chopped mango

¾ ounce mixed mint and cilantro leaves

This salad is full of carotenoids, which protect against heart disease, in particular beta-carotene, an antioxidant that protects cells and reduces the risk of cancer.

AZ *Alkalizing* **D** *Digestion Boosting* **SR** *Skin Repairing*

Place the dressing in the bottom of a quart jar. Add the green onions, followed by the brown rice, carrot, butternut squash, mango, and, finally, the mint and cilantro leaves. Seal the jar tightly.

ROASTED CAULIFLOWER

Makes: 1 quart — Time: 25 minutes

YOU NEED

2 to 4 tablespoons Tahini Zinger (page 18) • 2 green onions, thinly sliced
1 Persian cucumber, sliced • 1¾ ounces radishes, sliced
½ cup cooked or canned chickpeas • 3½ ounces roasted cauliflower
4½ ounces Swiss chard, stems removed and leaves finely chopped

This contains dietary nitrates, which have been shown to improve muscle oxygenation during exercise, which in turn builds endurance.

AI *Anti-inflammatory* **ME** *Mineral Enhancing* **BS** *Blood Sugar Stabilizing*

Place the dressing in the bottom of a quart jar. Add the green onions, followed by the cucumber, radishes, chickpeas, cauliflower, and Swiss chard. Seal the jar tightly.

GREEK SALAD

Makes: 1 quart — Time: 10 minutes

YOU NEED

2 to 3 tablespoons Red Wine Vinaigrette (page 28, with ½ teaspoon dried
oregano added) • ½ small red onion, very finely sliced • ½ cup cooked or
canned chickpeas • 3 ounces cherry tomatoes, halved • 3 ounces
Persian cucumber, chopped • 1¾ ounces pitted Kalamata olives • 1 ounce feta
cheese, crumbled • 2¾ ounces Little Gem lettuce, chopped

This salad is full of hydrating and anti-inflammatory ingredients.

HD *Hydrating* **AI** *Anti-inflammatory* **D** *Digestion Boosting*

Place the vinaigrette in the bottom of a quart jar. Add the
red onion, followed by the chickpeas, tomatoes, cucumber,
olives, feta, and, finally, the lettuce. Seal the jar tightly.

SWEET AND CREAMY QUINOA

Makes: 1 quart — Time: 15 minutes

YOU NEED

¼ cup hummus • 1 teaspoon extra-virgin olive oil

¼ cup cooked or canned black beans • ½ cup cooked and seasoned

red and white quinoa • ½ small orange, segmented

½ small avocado, peeled, pitted, and sliced • 1 ounce lacinato kale, chopped

A handful of sprouts (such as lentil, chickpea, alfalfa, broccoli)

This is packed with vitamin C, which is essential for repairing damaged tissues, fighting off free radicals (which may play a role in heart disease), and fighting colds.

I *Immune Boosting* **BR** *Blood Regulating* **BF** *Bacteria Fighting*

Place the hummus in the bottom of a quart jar. Drizzle over the oil.
Add the black beans, followed by the quinoa, orange segments,
avocado, kale, and, finally, the sprouts. Seal the jar tightly.

SHIITAKE, CRANBERRIES, AND LENTILS

Makes: 1 quart – Time: 25 minutes

YOU NEED

2 tablespoons French Vinaigrette (page 20) • ¾ cup cooked Puy lentils
A small handful of chervil leaves • 3½ ounces small shiitake mushrooms
(with stems attached), roasted • 1 ounce goat cheese, crumbled • 1 ounce dried
cranberries • 1 ounce mixed baby greens • 2 tablespoons chopped toasted almonds

This salad is a great iron booster. Iron is essential, necessary for transporting oxygen throughout the body.

D *Digestion Boosting* **B** *Blood Stimulating* **E** *Energizing*

Place the vinaigrette in the bottom of a quart jar. Add the lentils and chervil and stir to coat. Add the shiitake mushrooms, then the goat cheese, cranberries, baby greens, and, finally, the almonds. Seal the jar tightly.

SWEET ENDINGS

*Breakfasts, desserts, and snacks—take
your pick; this chapter covers them all.
These jars are full of grains, protein-rich
yogurt, fruits, and seeds to fill you up
whatever the time of day. Because these
recipes all contain fresh fruits, they are
best consumed within twenty-four hours.*

OVERNIGHT OATS

Makes: 1¼ cups — Time: 10 minutes, plus standing

YOU NEED

⅓ cup rolled oats • 6 tablespoons fresh apple juice
1 ounce dried fruit, chopped • 3 tablespoons plain yogurt (reduced fat or fat-free
is fine) • 1¾ ounces apple, chopped • 2 tablespoons chopped nuts
1 teaspoon maple syrup

The oats are a terrific source of manganese, essential for bones, skin health, blood sugar control, and protecting against cell damage.

D *Digestion Boosting* **E** *Energizing* **BS** *Blood Sugar Stabilizing*

Place the oats in the bottom of a small jar. Add the apple juice and then the dried fruit and mix to combine. Leave for 15 minutes, or overnight. Add the yogurt, apple, chopped nuts, and maple syrup. Seal the jar tightly.

PLUM PARFAIT

Makes: 1¼ cups — Time: 20 minutes

YOU NEED

2 large plums, pitted and cut into 12 slices

1 tablespoon coconut sugar • 2 tablespoons water

⅔ cup plain Greek yogurt (reduced fat or fat-free is fine) • 1 ounce granola

The plums increase your body's ability to absorb iron, and Greek yogurt is a great source of protein and probiotics.

BF *Bacteria Fighting* **HS** *Hunger Suppressing* **BS** *Blood Sugar Stabilizing*

In a small saucepan, cook the plums with the coconut sugar and water until the plums are softened and the liquid is syrupy. Layer in a small jar with the yogurt. Cut a small square of parchment paper, place directly on top of the plums, and add the granola. Seal the jar tightly.

COCONUT, CHIA, AND BERRY JAR

Makes: 1¼ cups — Time: 5 minutes

YOU NEED

1 tablespoon chia seeds • 6 tablespoons light coconut milk

¼ cup fresh shredded coconut • 2 teaspoons honey

A small handful of raspberries • A small handful of blueberries

The chia seeds are a superfood: filling and full of fiber, omega-3 fats, antioxidants, and protein.

 *Strengthening*  *Blood Regulating*  *Hunger Suppressing*

Place the chia seeds in a small jar. Add the coconut milk, shredded coconut, and honey and stir to combine. Top with the raspberries and blueberries. Seal the jar tightly.

QUINOA AND BLACKBERRY BOWL

Makes: 1¼ cups — Time: 5 minutes

YOU NEED

½ cup plain Greek yogurt (reduced fat or fat-free is fine) • ½ cup blackberries
⅓ cup cooked red and white quinoa • ½ cup dried apricots, chopped
2 teaspoons mixed seeds (such as pumpkin and sunflower) • 1 teaspoon honey

This is full of magnesium, which is essential for heart health and the absorption of calcium for bone health.

HS *Hunger Suppressing* **BPL** *Blood Pressure Lowering* **BS** *Blood Sugar Stabilizing*

Place the yogurt in a small jar. Add the blackberries, quinoa, and dried apricots. Finish with the mixed seeds and honey. Seal the jar tightly.

TROPICAL FRUIT MIX-UP

Makes: 1¼ cups — Time: 10 minutes

YOU NEED

1 teaspoon lime zest plus 1 tablespoon lime juice • 1 teaspoon coconut sugar
2 ounces peeled, pitted, and chopped mango • 2 ounces peeled seedless
watermelon, chopped • 1 small peeled kiwi fruit, chopped
2 ounces peeled banana, chopped • A small handful of shredded coconut

The coconut sugar contains nutrients such as zinc and iron as well as antioxidants, making it a healthier choice than granulated sugar.

HD *Hydrating* **H** *Healing* **IF** *Infection Fighting*

Place the lime zest, lime juice, and coconut sugar in the bottom of a small jar and stir to dissolve the sugar. Layer in the mango, watermelon, kiwi, and banana. Finish with the coconut. Seal the jar tightly.

DATE, STRAWBERRY, AND BRAZIL NUT JAR

Makes: 1¼ cups – Time: 10 minutes

YOU NEED

3 Medjool dates, pitted • ⅓ cup plain yogurt (reduced fat or
fat-free is fine) • 3 ounces strawberries, hulled and quartered
¾ ounce mixed toasted Brazil nuts and shelled pistachios

This is a great source of selenium for metabolic health, fertility, cognitive function, and a healthy immune system.

 **S** *Strengthening* **D** *Digestion Boosting* **MS** *Metabolic Support*

Purée the dates with 1 tablespoon of warm water until very smooth, then place in the bottom of a small jar. Add the yogurt, followed by the strawberries, Brazil nuts, and pistachios. Seal the jar tightly.

INDEX

Originally published in French in France as *Shaker Salades: La Bible* by Marabout,
a member of Hachette Livre, Paris, in 2015. Copyright © 2015 by Hachette Livre
(Marabout)

Library of Congress Cataloging-in-Publication Data is on file with the publisher.

Trade Paperback ISBN: 978-0-399-57937-0
eBook ISBN: 978-0-399-57938-7

Printed in China

Design by Alice Chadwick
Photography by Victoria Wall Harris

10 9 8 7 6 5 4 3 2 1

First American Edition

ACKNOWLEDGMENTS

Thank you a hundred times over to Catie Ziller, Kathy Steer, Alice Chadwick,
Victoria Wall Harris, and Anna Shillinglaw Hampton. Thank you also to Bob's
Red Mill for providing me with all of the grains to test these recipes with, and to
Kuhn Rikon for sorting me out with a great salad spinner and slicing set to work
with. Finally, to my husband, Don, who ate salad upon salad for breakfast, lunch,
and dinner and never once complained.